## Extreme Overflow Publishing

A division of Extreme Overflow Enterprises, Inc
Grayson, Georgia 30017
www.extremeoverflow.com

Copyright ©2014
Edited by Extreme Overflow Publishing
Front Cover design & layout by Extreme Overflow Publishing
www.extremeoverflow.com
Photography Credit: Glamour Shots

*Extreme Overflow Publishing titles may be purchased in bulk for educational, business, fundraising, or sales promotional use. For information, please email*
info@extreme-overflow-enterprises.com.

Unless otherwise noted, all Scripture quotations are taken from the Life Application Study Bible, New International Version.

Manufactured in the United States of America
10  9  8  7  6  5  4  3  2  1

ISBN: 978-0-9885998-8-8

A LEADER'S GUIDE TO ACHIEVING AND

SUSTAINING EXCELLENCE

# Next

# LEVEL UP

REVAMPING THE BLUEPRINT OF SUCCESSFUL
ENTREPRENEURSHIP

# CONTENTS

# Introduction

Anything you do starts with a day 1. Whether it is a diet, an exercise routine, a new school, a business or whether you're building your house of success; it all starts with a day 1.

## WHAT"S KEEPING YOU FROM YOUR DAY 1?

For many the problem is that you're thinking too small. When you think small everything you do will look just as small as you feared it would. If you're going to operate, manage and reap all of the benefits of successful entrepreneurship, you can't be afraid and surely you can't think small. Goal attainment isn't a task for the weak at heart, nor is it for the impatient. But with passion, a made up mind and focus you can build the success house of your wildest dreams! And if you already have a success house built, it's time to take it to the NEXT LEVEL UP!

## WHAT IS A SUCCESS HOUSE?

A "success house" is different than your

"dream home." A dream home is the place where you stop, rest and admire all of your hard work. But your success house is the place in your mind, heart and soul that expands! It is the place where at the very thought of your goal, your entire being just goes crazy inside with excitement. It not only reaches but is built and equipped to attain whatever goal you decide to go after. Unlike your dream home filled with accolades and accomplishments of the past, your success house is filled with things that have yet to be achieved; the balance of humble entrepreneurship at its finest.

## AS A LEADER HOW DO I TAKE MY LIFE TO THE NEXT LEVEL UP?

From this book you will learn how to revamp the design of your success house and scale it to accommodate everything you wish to accomplish as a leader in business and MORE. By the end of this book, you will know that you CAN do it (whatever "it" may be for you)! What you will also find in this book are the tips, tools and secrets to establishing your personal definitions of success, peace, and confidence as a business leader.

## WHAT IS THE NEXT LEVEL UP?

So you're ready for change, you say, right?

9

Perhaps you're in an uncomfortable place right now; though on the path to the palace. You can see the palace, smell it and feel how close you are to it, but you're still in transition, right? The next level up starts with a place of vision. What makes the next level up a tad bit complex is that it sees the goal but feels the differential between the present status; the path, and the palace. However, no matter what kind of transition you may be experiencing how you respond to this place of transition is what will release you into the next level up; the place of destiny.

The Next level up is also about a movement. Sometimes this transition involves you moving out of something. Other times you might just be moving into something, or even away from someone; all equivalent to the next level up. Simply put, the next level up is a about a progression from your current location to the place of purpose.

Transition is not known to be easy. If anything it presents itself to be a rather difficult experience. For this reason many people plateau in their careers, businesses, academic pursuits, faith, and so on. Essentially because they are afraid of the challenges that come with moving into the uncomfortable new territory that they've asked for, the place they've always dreamed they could be in their personal and professional life.

But what happens is somewhere along their journey they lose their way. Maybe circumstance through them off track. Perhaps having children or getting married or divorced or a fight with a sister or brother or friend caught them off guard; and un-forgiveness and a lack of humility kept them from pursuing their assigned destiny. Due to this off track response the result forfeits the reward(s) that come with living on the next level; the place of freedom to walk out and walk in God-given purpose, not looking for anyone else's approval to do so.

You see, there's no room for keeping up with the "Jones" (whoever they are) on the next level up. As a matter of fact, instead of looking at the "Jones'" (who are not looking at you, by the way) get busy taking your own life to the next level up. No more seeing if the grass is greener on the other side of the fence. Get away from the window to the Jones's yard and do something about your own! There is only time, space, and energy for aligning your lifestyle to reach your destined purpose in business by taking your life to the NEXT LEVEL UP.

Focus. Defining, creating, recreating and revamping the blueprint of successful entrepreneurship is personal. It's different for everyone, which is why it can't be compared; it is also the reason why the neighborhood of business ownership is so beautiful.

Within every chapter of this book it is my hope that you are going to find yourself setting your mind on the next level up! As you read, use your imagination. Think about things in the literal context of building a house, at a very high level of course. For example, in the simplest form you know that before an architectural construct can be built there needs to first be a blueprint; Same concept applies to your personal goals as a leader and your business. Before any dream is fulfilled, before any movement of change occurs there must be a blueprint. It is imperative to know how you're going to get there; which path is right for you, before you achieve the next level up.

## WHY A BLUEPRINT?

When building a house, the first step is to make sure that you have created the blueprint before any materials are bought or before any construction occurs. The reason is because the blueprint is what helps the builders to know what size, how many dimensions the house has, windows, doors, elevations and so on. So as it relates to your own entrepreneurial endeavors, it won't matter how good your blueprint looks in your mind or how enthusiastic you are about your plan if you're too afraid to execute it. And walking out destiny without a blueprint should make you afraid . . . .very afraid! Even God designed the heavens and earth with a plan for purpose, how much then should you consider the same?

## ARE YOU WILLING TO PAY THE COST?

Maybe you've tried to do this in the past and nothing worked out as planned. Perhaps you feel insecure because your efforts seemed to produce failure and not results. Those feelings are indeed real. But, guess what? Those moments of failure are probably the best thing that could have ever happened to you.

## WHY?

. . . because failure in keeping up your business empire is like taking a dose of medicine. While it may have left a gross taste in your mouth, it has made you a better, more motivated, more dedicated, more committed, and more driven leader in your field! None of which could have been formulated in any other way. None of which could have gotten you to be ready to shift to the next level up like you are today! Your experiences; the good and bad, are valuable. Never forget their value. Don't be embarrassed by them, learn and move forward. There isn't any part of your journey that will be perfect and that's what makes it perfect! At the end of the day when it's all said and done, everything works out as an instrument to something better in your future. Remember that when things don't work out as planned and you can't hear or see what you know God promised to you, trust that you are still exactly where you're supposed to be; in a position of growing success!

## HOW DO YOU KNOW THIS?

First things first, I don't claim to know all of anything. But what I learn along the way I share in hopes that it will help someone else get to where they're trying to go, a little bit faster or with a little more wisdom.

I too am a mother to two beautiful sons, a wife of a loving husband, who has had to create my own blueprint for successful entrepreneurship through a lifestyle my family and I could stand to live out together. Just like you! I have moonlighted for years trying to build, discover, and implement the things I love to do, some things I even held off doing because I was afraid, but not anymore. In the end I finally trusted God to guide me and "wallah," the blue print was created! I say "wallah" as if it were easy, but it wasn't. It was actually pretty hard!

Nonetheless, I enjoy the duties, challenges, and responsibilities of being a mother and wife, but don't get it twisted-it is the most rewarding, fulfilling and difficult work I've ever done! So whoever tells you it is easy to run a business and have a family whether they have 1 child or 8 children, lied to you! Don't listen to anything else they have to say!

Fulfilling my call, role, status and value as a mother and wife who is also a business owner has in many cases been perplexed by the attainment of reaching my goals and other aspirations; what I felt I was led to do. But through all of the tears, loss of friends, change in finances, places to live, jobs, and anything else you can imagine, I am blessed to have my family and a core team of individuals who dust me off when I have fallen. Who cheer me on when I succeed and who tell me the truth when I need to hear it most. For this, I am thankful. God has been more than good to me and my family. So today, one life at a time I strive to help others walk out their dreams. Therefore it is my hope that you will embrace what is shared in this book. And if you learn nothing new, it is my hope that you will pass this information on to someone who will benefit. They will thank you later. I bid to you many blessings in abundance as your strive to know that your future is LIMITLESS!

# FOUNDATION

## ...A builder mindset

*I have a mind to build and manage a successful business.*

# *What or who is in your head?*

# Chapter 1

*Are you afraid that your idea will be the
success you imagine?*

## IDENTIFYING FEARS OF SUCCESS

So, you're sitting on the couch in your living
room watching television. As your mind wanders
you recall all of the moments you pretended to be

on television growing up. Maybe you even went to college for it. It was your dream, your passion, your purpose for living. This dream was the very air you breathed. But now today as you watch the television it would appear that person you're looking at stole that dream from you; they are living out the success of you always wanted to live while you're on the couch in your bath robe waiting on dinner to finish cooking!

Look at them! They're you're age, shape, height and everything! How could this have happened, you might be thinking? Where did I let go of that vision? Think about it, when did you stop believing you could do it?

Attaining the level of success you've only dreamed of for your life begins with a vision. Vision involves activating your emotions as well as your mind. It is more than a rationale and cannot be predicted, but is essential to planning strategically to obtain it. It holds hands with commitment, and is birthed out of what was planted or implanter in your mind over the years. The power in the growth of your vision is driven by a relentless pursuit and desire to make it happen.

## GOT VISION?

You may or may not know or have realized this, but your mind is powerful. William James once said that, "There is a law in psychology that states, if you form a picture in your mind of what you would like to be, and you keep and hold that picture there long enough, you will soon become exactly as you have been thinking." What he was expressing was the power of thought. How you allow your mind to think about your dream; as it relates to being a leader in business ownership, has the potential to increase creativity and productivity for all that you do. But on the other hand it also has the power to tear down the very idea of you owning your own business to where it will never come to fruition.

Through the vehicle of fear, a negative mindset toward judging your ability to run a business successfully can keep the idea of business ownership from ever happening in your life. Your mind is indeed that powerful. For this reason successful entrepreneurship starts with a decision to do it. For example let's say you are a person who loves books but you work at the corporate office of one of the largest firms in the country. You are doing it big time with your own corner office and wall of windows; you've got it made! But let's say you decide to pursue your passion for books. Full commitment to this passion would require you to work hard. Possibly even leave your current job, move to the countryside and open up a quaint book store coffee shop. As brave as that decision would be, your mind amongst the support of your family and friends, would probably ask if you were "sure" this is what you really wanted to do; as if you were making the wrong decision or something. But is there anything really wrong with following your passion?

## WHAT HAS YOUR MIND OR FRIENDS OR FAMILY CONVINCED YOU THAT YOU CANNOT DO?

In order to see this passion to fruition you would have to convince your mind to see beyond the simple notion of opening up a book store. Going even further, your mind would need to agree that you would be ok and happy doing it. Your mind would need to agree to be proud to define it as successful. Do you let your mind do that? When was the last time you told yourself its ok to go to where you're aspiring to grow to in business? On the contrary, it is your passion, why wouldn't you go for it? When you reflect on the reasons of why or why not, everything you ever wanted lies on the other side of that fear.

Sure there are many outliers that would need to be configured depending upon the complex dynamics of your individual situation. Nonetheless, the power your mind has over this one decision could very well be the lever to the door of opportunity you've always be looking for; the door that brings you from a life of mediocrity to a life of success on the next level up.

Success is defined by many. However, there is only one definition of success that truly matters. It is the one you create for yourself. So, what's your definition of success? Think about what success looks like for you. Does success look like the person with the most degrees? Does it look like the man or woman with the biggest house or largest bank account? What is success to you? The answer is that success is what you make of it. For some being a great mother is a success, especially if you didn't get the chance to have one. For others being awarded the employee of the month is a success or having a baby is a success, owning your own business is a success, and the list of things that make a person successful can go on forever. Success is and can only be defined by you; never lost in the sauce of someone else's expectations.

To be perfectly clear, success is not defined as everyone running their own business, either. Don't worry you are not the only one who may have thought that to be true. Business ownership is a form of success, but it is not the only kind of success you can have in life. However, if business ownership is something you've ever considered, wouldn't it be fun to measure up to it?

On the next few pages you will find a fun quiz that is purposed to assess your skill level for entrepreneurship. Inspired by Glamour Magazine[1], take a moment to see if you have what it takes to start a business.

---

[1] Glamour.com/inspired

## QUIZ- ENTREPRENEUR DNA; Do you have it?

### Part 1: Puzzles

Select the missing design from the options on the right to replace the question mark on the left.

**No. 1**

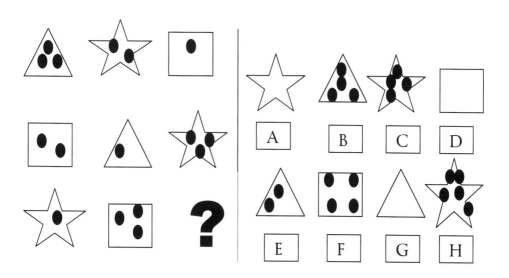

Part 2: Personality

For each pair of statements below, select the one that describes you the best. Both may be true, but which is most you?

**No. 2**

    A.  I have a good word for everyone.

    B.  I carry the conversation to a higher level.

**No. 3**

    A.  I have a vivid imagination.

    B.  I pay attention to details.

**No. 4**

    A.  I get excited by new ideas.

    B.  I'm not easily bothered by things.

**No. 5**

    A.  I believe that others have good intentions.

    B.  I have a rich vocabulary.

**No. 6**

    A.  I make friends easily.

    B.  I can say things beautifully.

Scoring Yourself

For each of the following answers give yourself one point.

Answers: 1,e; 2,b; 3,a; 4,a; 5,b; 6,b

## IF YOU GOT....

### 5-6 POINTS

You're a natural entrepreneur! You have the curiosity and originality necessary to challenge accepted norms and you can quickly solve complex problems in a constantly changing playing field.

### 3-4 POINTS

You'd succeed either in a larger company or at starting your own. To improve your entrepreneurial skills attend start up events and share your ideas with potential clients.

### BELOW 3 POINTS

You would do better as part of a team as opposed to leading it.

Keep in mind that there is no right or wrong answer to this quiz. It was included here as a fun assessment of personality and entrepreneurial skill; one of the many out there. That being said, how'd you do? What did you learn about yourself? Did you find that you were a natural born leader?

## MODERN LEADERSHIP

The definition of leadership has been studied for quite some time amongst a plethora of scholars. The concept of leadership was introduced in the early 1800's (Fairholm & Fairholm, 2009). Rather than look at the past efforts of what leadership has been defined as, the time to draw new conceptualizations of leadership that provide better and more thorough grasps of this difficult to understand social experience, is now. In this generation we've reached a place where opportunity is possible for anyone. In some cases, there is almost more supply than there is demand. Nonetheless, many call themselves leaders; with no idea the power and impact leadership has. If we do not unearth new ways to adapt, train and raise up true leaders who serve in true leadership, no matter the age, will excavate the demise of our cultural society entirely. Integrating leadership principles of the past to apply to today's narcissistic attitudes of leadership might prove to be near impossible. But that's where the blueprint comes in. Rethinking and redefining the substance of what makes a person a leader, defining their leadership style and ethics in a manner that is intriguing, engaging, potent, and unique is the establishment of your blueprint.

## DEFINING MINDSETS

Using the previous quiz was fun. But whether you scored as an entrepreneur or not, thousands of individuals think it is easy to become an entrepreneurial leader because of how the output looks. But it's not easy. Anything worth having is worth working hard for. It's important that you know this before you start creating, dreaming, wishing, hoping and so on. You CAN have all that you're mind can imagine, just know that it will not be easy to acquire it.

*"Anything worth having is worth working for."*

ARE YOU STILL UP FOR THE CHALLENGE?

According to the Bureau of Labor Statistics[2], the number of people who quit their jobs in September 2014 were up .3 million since the previous month of August. Why do you think these people are quitting? They still have to eat, pay bills and so forth, so how are they going to make it? Self employment is on the rise. More than ever people believe in an alternate path through self employment. The self employment rates are high and increasing with low decline of unincorporated statuses. This data can be interpreted to extrapolate that people are finding a way to create the life they want. However, without realizing it an entrepreneur can easily spend 60 or more hours a week devising strategies, designing new products, services, mulling around ideas, brainstorming, streamlining operational activities and managing people. And if that wasn't enough by itself, others are moonlighting. Needless to say it takes a tireless amount of effort to run a company of any size. But if you can get to a place where you love what you do; revamping the blueprint of your leadership as needed, those hours will fly by and never seem like there is enough because the wheels in the mind of an

---

[2] Bureau of Labor Statistics, U.S. Department of Labor, *The Economics Daily*, Hires and quits increase in September 2014

entrepreneur are always turning. Contrarily, and as great as this all sounds, if you're mind has been telling you you'll never get there, and you believe it-you won't.

Previous experience can easily cause the strongest of persons to doubt the possibility of ever reaching a goal or ever trying again. But you must. One of the things that can help you to reframe your mind to believe that you can accomplish whatever you set your mind to do; despite any respite of failure, is to evaluate your current mindset. Knowing your mindset is the first step in learning how to set your mind on things above; on better things.

Research has concluded an assortment of ways to dissect and break out entrepreneurial mindset traits[3]; nonetheless, here you will find the pertinent mind and personality traits compacted in three straightforward components. As you read through the distinct differences between all three, the *Glower*, the *Show-er*, and the *Grower*, see if there is one that best fits how you think in terms of business.

Meet "Ms. Glow"

---

[3] fi.co/dna

The Glower frame of mind thinks adventurously! This type of leader is a forward thinking individual who tends to be rather outgoing. They love to network. When they walk in a room the room stops to stare and listens because of their glowing presence. Their graceful confidence employs their excitement and action oriented nature. They enjoy working with people and have the ability to be determined in self discipline.

Meet "Ms. Show"
The Show-er frame of mind, lives by the motto, "show and prove." This leader has a strong aptitude for problem solving. They drive the delivery of products and other releases on time. They have a strong business sense and allow their intellect to guide them in leadership.

Meet "Ms. Grow"
The Grower frame of mind is a highly creative and tactical think tank. This leader is full of bright ideas; they never stop flowing. Almost annoying to most they are people who are constantly on the look-out for new ways to do things and put them into action. Because of their agility they lead well in demanding scenarios without letting hardship bring them down.

WHICH FRAME OF MIND ARE YOU?

Each frame of mind in leadership has its proper place in your business career. The goal in identifying your mindset is for the benefit of understanding how you grow or have not been growing in your business. So, did you find areas that are either missing in yourself as the leader? During your reflection you may have identified that you have a grower frame of mind but realize the need for a little more of a show-mentality. When you take the time to identify the gaps in your thinking, it makes it easier to fill the voids of lack which in turn will help you to create strong business operations and improve the development of your entrepreneurial blueprint. Improvement from the inside; your mind, is what will maintain steady increase of your business successes and keep your entrepreneurial dream alive.

## THEY WILL FOLLOW WHEN THEY SEE TRUE LEADERSHIP

Most of the research on leadership focuses on the dynamics of leadership rather than it's personality. Being the type of leader that drives success and creates results is more than just telling people what to do. There is a personal, intimate penchant to defining true leadership and then authenticate this leadership to convert into mechanics that work for today's culture. For this reason you will find more current research focusing in on the behavioral aspect of leadership development. As you are creating the blueprint for your leadership success it is important for you to not only develop, "Here's the plan," but to build on this growing body of research by employing the leadership strategies presented in this book. The models and tactics within were created and presented to you as a template to generate comprehensive understanding of the personality of leadership in a way that will transcend to mental perceptions and physical attributes of you as a dynamic leader. The importance of these principles impacts the maturation or death of your business.

*"...The beauty surrounding the revamp of your entrepreneurial blueprint entails you setting your own path to success!"*

## DREAM KILLERS

Did you know that you can kill the manifestation of your own dream just by thinking you can't do it or by thinking that it might not happen? Yes, YOU! Not situations, haters or circumstances. You are you're one and only dream killer!

Even after the people talk and the haters hate, your response is what changes things or keeps them the same. When you believe negative thought; focusing on all the ways it can't work instead of all the ways it just might, you cut off the air your dream needs to breathe; to come to fruition.

Think back to the first day you decided to start your business? You were excited, right? You probably started that dream at the finish line too; operating a successful establishment or providing stellar services to large corporations, right? While sometimes slightly unrealistic for a start, it is completely normal to dream and dream big. With enough gall, the right tools and resources all of what you envision can all very well come true.

Most career or personal goals start with a dream; a vision of yourself in the place you want to be. Additionally, most visions necessitate their beginning with a blueprint; an action plan to get you there. Maybe you dreamt that dream before marriage or before kids, it can still happen, you know? There is no better time than the present to create an action plan. Today is the opportunity you've been waiting for to do so. The best part about you being able to revamp your blueprint now is that you get to design it to fit into your current lifestyle as a wiser, stronger and more experienced individual.

Your action plan shouldn't ever make you feel like you're being forced into a career path or a business direction that is set by someone else. The beauty surrounding the revamp of your entrepreneurial blueprint entails you setting your own path to success! The one that includes you loving what you do, enjoying time with family and taking time for yourself. Living out your dream does not equate to the forfeit of what is important.

Instead it can compliment a balance of you being able to enjoy every minute of time you have with those you love.

So you've tried this before and it didn't work-got it! However there is something you may not have known back when you tried to redesign the accomplishment of your business goals the first time. Here's the kicker: You were born to carry out what is inside of you. You can't ignore it. Not anymore! There are people waiting for you to burst out in the song and dance of your dream! You can't kill it and surely you cannot let it die inside of you. Your contribution to this world is what makes you beautiful, it's what makes your company stronger and it's what makes the world a better place.

### THERE IS POWER IN THE BLUEPRINT

Creating a blueprint for your entrepreneurial life will aid in the development of discovering your personal leadership skills, clearly define who you are in business, what your product or talent is as well as challenge your personal courage to make it happen. You must do and learn to focus on reframing your mind, to know the difference between what you want, what you're naturally good at and what someone else wants you to do. There is power in the latter.

The next level up blueprint is full of divine power. It believes in who you are before you actually become it. The power of the blueprint is a natural sense of constant design; the blueprint craves God's way which is happiness, peace, love and the enjoyment of life. The power of the blueprint will pull and tug on you in the middle of the night, while you're taking your shower or cooking; it will hit you right upside your head. All of sudden you have a great idea and have to stop what you're doing and write it down. That moment right there is the power of the blueprint. Has that ever happened to you before? You might have thought you were crazy by it! Don't worry, you're not crazy. You were just struck by the power of the blueprint!

As you consider your design and need for redesigning, evolving, and deepening the complexities and dimensions of how you're going to reach your business goals things can almost feel like the walls are either caving in around you or that everything about where you're trying to go has become completely overwhelming. That's normal. It's not easy to be a leader. There are moments even amidst all your bright ideas, you wonder if you are qualified enough to carry it out. You wonder if you can get up enough money or get connected to the right people, and the list goes on. The more you understand about where you're going is sometime the more you can find yourself in a place of fear. Fear doesn't mean you lack faith as long as you don't let it kill the dream; don't be a dream killer. When those feelings arise, you may just need to take a break, step away and organize the racing of your thoughts. When you've settled yourself down and stop focusing on the self sabotaging what ifs, you can get out that pen and paper, text yourself, record yourself, or whatever your vice to accountability, continue to write the vision; make it plain. If you don't, it probably won't leave you alone, until you do. The power of the blueprint is relentless in its pursuit for you because that great idea you are doing your best to write on paper is heaven sent! You have heaven's support and God's approval to accomplish that great idea. No matter how deep you are into starting or mastering your blueprint and no matter what may come your way as a distraction in the process (oh boy will things come!), keep moving toward the goal. It's going to get tough. Revamping, improving, and building won't come easy. But anything worth having is worth working for. So whatever you do, don't kill the dream!

## POSITIVE TALK

Studies show that entrepreneurial behavior is positively linked to emotional intelligence. Entrepreneurial behavior is defined by a series of actions that seek to take advantage of opportunities that have either gone unnoticed or have not been fully vetted (Bahadori, 2012). This means that as an entrepreneur your eyes are always on the lookout for ways to improve the way things are being done. Or are otherwise innovating new ways to get it done. The trigger and first line processer to those actions being carried out; in addition to having the idea and the people, are how you manage your emotional intelligence.

## WHAT IS EMOTIONAL INTELLIGENCE?

Emotional intelligence is the way you think and feel about yourself. The effects of your thoughts eventually turn into words. Those words eventually turn into what you do or don't do; all of which are influenced by what you think and feel about yourself.

As an entrepreneurial leader, what you tell yourself about yourself is what you will see in your business. Therefore if you think low about yourself, your business will reflect that. Moreover, that is what your employees, partners, investors, and customers will see; which will not keep them interested for long. Why should they believe in you or your product, if you don't?

## PARADIGM SHIFT

The importance of configuring a new business corporation is growing daily within various organizational structures, lending itself to every area of business; innovative product line development, service offerings and creating lean processes. This is how you shift, by building strong business processes that enable a constant developmental environment.

Nowadays, an organization's environment has become diverse as it has dynamic. Now more than ever, managers and leaders are looking for ways to create or enhance their competitive advantages and unique nature. In the revamp of a leader's blueprint to success understanding your entrepreneurial intelligence, thought life, and mindset can help you facilitate rapid change and innovation.

## DEFINING MOMENTS

As you mature personally and professionally other things in your life change also. One of the things that change is when you assume greater positional authority and responsibility whether it's at work or by getting married, having children, and the list goes on. However leadership is about making decisions on policies, changes, and the like that at the end of the day will help you get things done more efficiently. More than a change in style or approach these decisions are founded from a design, a blueprint of what your success looks like going forward. How will your success be achieved given the shift in responsibility, authority or position in your life? For example when your child is sick from school and you have a meeting planned, what do you do? What if in the middle of things getting really good for you in business, right before an event, your spouse gets sick needing hospital attention immediately, what do you do? As it relates to creating your personal blueprint, think about your business or the businesses you want to create and ask yourself the following:

1. What is your current business state of mind?

2. Do you know the needs of your target market?

3. What makes what you do or what you want to do differently spectacular?

4. What are you passionate about?

5. What skills do you currently have?

6. What does your company or your desired industry need and value?

These questions are designed to help you consider your own blueprint and have conviction about your passion; your business. Take a moment

to explore your passion and research ideas tied to
it for six to ten hours a week. Give yourself about
8 weeks to come up with an idea viable enough to
start developing; an idea that will take your life to
the next level up.

# FRAMING

## ...Specs & Details

*My leadership is true and authentic.*

# *The Plan*

# Chapter 2

WHAT KIND OF LEADER ARE YOU?

## AUTHENTIC LEADERSHIP

Authentic leadership positively shapes the many aspects of organizational behavior. There are two very important things to note about authenticity. The first is that authenticity is not an imitation of anything. It's unique, original and often times stands out. There is no way to be authentic and copy someone else at the same time. Authenticity is about being *you*. Naturally, you must first figure out who that is first before you can authentically lead anything or anyone.

The second important point about authenticity is accepting what makes you different. As a leader, you cannot be ashamed of the fact that you are and might do things a little different than the next leader; being different is a beautiful thing. As it relates to discovering your authentic leader abilities, there is one requirement to follow. That is to be committed to your personal development. Taking risks are equivalent to investing in your future. Let yourself make mistakes and learn from them. It's the idea of marrying yourself to your passion and making it your profession. As with any newlywed relationship, there will be mistakes made, but what you learn from them is what builds the relationship. Through this coupling of commitment and growth, is an expressed responsibility that is devoted toward realizing the longevity of your potential in leadership. Novelist

*"The story of your life is not your life. It is your story."*

*-John Barth*

John Barth said it best, "The story of your life is not your life. It is your story." Your story knits the fabric of your experiences which later becomes the perception of yourself and your leadership. You can either view yourself as the victim and your situation helpless or you can decide to rise above the situation and view yourself as an opportune leader.

You may have been a person that has experienced multiple setbacks, a tumultuous child hood, and a neglected and rejected adulthood. You may have even been lied on and lied to on more than one occasion, discriminated against, left out and the list goes on. However, if you can overcome those things, these are the types of experiences that can make for great leader material. That is only when you can find a way to extract meaning from every morsel of every experience. A leader finds a way to motivate themselves through their challenges by capturing their true passion within; which essentially motivates others.

Leadership emerges from your life's story. However what you must be careful of is being tricked by its power. Those experiences typically are the fuel to your drive toward success. Your drive alone can enable you to be professionally successful for a while but drive alone will not be able to sustain your success as a leader. Don't be fooled. Don't be mashed into a box that drives results without authentic personality in your leadership style, because your authentic leadership is best exposed in your willingness to be vulnerable.

The proclivity of your vulnerability will radiate strength. Strength that others may be envious of, intimidated or even offended by. The blurred lines of a leader's authentic strength can be confusing to delineate due to roaring emotions of others or from within. As a result it can even cause blind spots in your leadership approach. For example, no matter how awesome you are as a leader or nice you are as a person, everyone is not going to like you or agree with your style. The sooner you can accept this the sooner you will be able to confidently cross over into authentic leadership. There will be times that you won't be able to smile big enough for people; nothing will be good enough for them. Nonetheless, trying to diminish the light your presence exudes won't help the situation either. Such action can be misinterpreted as fake. As a leader you don't want to be associated with fake.

Another blind spot can be as simple as acting too quickly to those who just don't care for your style anyway; this too will cripple your leadership capacities and abilities. So what can you do to avoid those feelings of rejection as a leader? How do you build such protection (an alarm system) into the design of your blueprint? The answer is in being honest. Accepting the fact that everyone will not be supportive toward your efforts only leaves room for you to grow into a stronger leader; accept it. In a perfect world, everyone will appreciate your contribution as a leader and will be excited for your success. A part of creating your blueprint is to be ready for reality. You see, denial can be the greatest hurdle that a leader faces in becoming self aware. Therefore a leader will need to have skin tough enough to endure hearing unwelcomed or unwarranted feedback they really don't want to hear and still be able to serve the vision and the people earnestly without any rollercoaster of negative emotions.

When your success, your career, or even your life hangs in the balance of what other people think of you, it can interrupt your leader thought of being able to authenticate what is most important and what you're prepared to sacrifice in order to create synergy between your personal feelings and your personal strength as a leader. This means you need to have a clear view of not only who you are but what's *really* important to you. This will help you to understand the health of your drive so you can take the value of your leadership and your team to the next level up!

## LEADERSHIP VALUES

The true essence of leadership is not in procedures per say. Instead, it is in the setting and teaching of values to followers. Programs, policies and procedures change, they always do. When they do the one thing that remains of your role as a leader is predicated on internalizing a consistent display of values.

One of the values of a leader is in their role as a leader. The role of a leader is enthusiastic in support of their people. On a level they demonstrate love, encouragement, enthusiasm, and inspiration to employees and others to maintain the organizations vision. As the leader they foster an innovative environment and are good about celebrating success. Doing so expands the scope of personal control that your workers can enjoy and collectively participate in for the betterment of the stakeholders, staff and employees.

Another value is a leader's focus. This value in leadership focuses on knowing how to work closely with a small core of direct reports; your leadership team. It is with this small cluster of folks that you as a leader get to practice your leadership. It is also within this cluster that the leader has the best opportunity to impact, change, and assist in the development of their peers.

Additionally, a leader's value is in its commitment to strive for development. Through follower trust, dedication and accountability, a leader's value in commitment is a process that continually measures itself against the vision of what the leader needs to do to remain true to it. Some of this is demonstrated in reports from the team and reflected in the health of the company.

The most significant mechanism for implementing a leader's value and purpose is the vision. The vision is the basis for everything the company does and its impact is an essential element to the power the vision holds through the leader. It is the force that binds the leader and follower together with common purpose; holy matrimony. Furthermore it is seen in the follower's and leader's actions, goal setting, prioritizing (personal and professional obligations) and all other conduct and decision making.

A leader's values also regulate the culture, of the organization. While the leader's past experiences, expectations for the future and personal values have shaped the leader's core, the display of the behavior following is what sets the tone for the rest of the organization. The hallmark of true leadership is coined by the ability to set and maintain a culture conducive to the follower's attainment of personal and organizational goals just as the leader has. Doing so establishes a standard for performance and behaviors.

Second to the vision, relationship lays congruent to the valued principles of true leadership. Followers must know and be able to feel not only your professionalism but must also feel a sense of personality and intimacy with you. Followers want to feel like they connect with whom they are following; by identifying even a piece of themselves or who they are striving to become.

Coaching is a fairly new concept of leadership (Fairholm & Fairholm, 2009). Even still it cannot be neglected in spelling out the leader's values. The very heart of coaching feeds the need for personal attention while empowering communication for the growth and development of your followers. Even if you are unable to meet and coach every single staff member you can foster an environment of coaching through self development that starts with you. It is important to develop strong leaders' other coaches because your cohorts are customarily volunteers. Therefore they must be coached in a way that inhabits everyone to see and experience results. The value in coaching within leadership, leads by example. It keeps the leader in a position of being teachable and in a position to teach and help grow others. Coaching can also help to develop a personal sense of loyalty toward your brand from those who look up to, work for and support your company.

There is a dual goal in leadership; developing self led staff and producing high performance output. The framework and technology in reaching this dual goal harvests the results the organization needs to sustain success. Therefore the measure of the value of success in your leadership is then defined by attaining both.

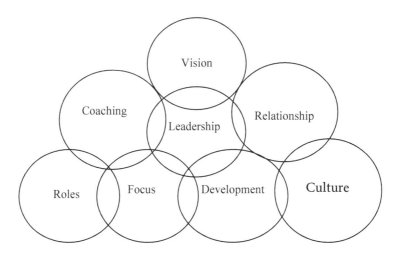

Figure 1: The Values of Leadership

## LEADERSHIP DISTINCTION

How you manage your values; what is important to you as a leader, is a reflection of your leadership distinctiveness; it is the character traits that separate your leadership style from someone else's. There are five traits that differentiate basic leadership from effective leadership. They are integrity, relevance, dominance, self confidence, and tolerance.

Integrity as a leadership trait maintains a standard of honesty with one's self and the people following. Integrity in leadership behaves ethically and is worthy of the teams confidence, trust and relevance.

Relevance as a leadership trait ensures the leader knows what has to be done and what resources are required for your organization to achieve its goals so that you can dominate your industry.

Dominance as a leadership trait does not walk around in the highest heels telling people what to do, although that is part of it. Nonetheless its main objective to dominance as a leadership trait ensures that the need to exert influence is not controlling, but rather helps to advocate the business toward the achievement of the organizations goal.

Self Confidence as a leadership trait motivates people. When you, as the leader, demonstrate confidence in how you dress, how you speak in public and about others only opens the door for people to be receptive to your influence. They are watching you. The least you can do is show them you love what you do by how you do it. Doing so will keep the organization energized with the perseverance needed to overcome obstacles and other day to day challenges.

Tolerance as a leadership trait has everything to do with being emotionally mature because it knows it has to tolerate stress and turn it into energy at a moment's notice! Tolerance or otherwise considered perseverance helps a leader deal with the uncertainties that come along with leadership; whether it is with the business or the people. It ensures the leader is able to manage the day to day demands with sensitivity and a mind for teamwork.

Effective leadership does not spend absorbing amounts of time in their feelings; being overly sensitive, self centered, insecure or unsure about their business. Instead leaders who are effective can control their feelings in any situation, manage the demands of day to day operations without negatively impacting the communication gateways between themselves, as the leader, and their team.

In reflection of yourself as a leader, do you find that you are missing any of these prominent leader traits? Which ones? How can you enhance the ones you're missing?

## LEADERSHIP IS ACTIVATED BY RELATIONSHIPS

Here's another standard of leadership, unless there is a relationship to cultivate there is no avenue to drive for results. In essence you cannot do what you do without the people who support and follow you. These same people need an interpersonal connection to you based on mutual respect and value in order to share in the loyalty of delivering results for the organization. Therefore leadership must be relational. Leadership is warmly welcoming and makes sure people are aware that they exist in a state of interconnectedness with all aspects of the business; working together to nourish and honor that relationship at all levels of activity.

Whether you'd like to admit it or not, leaders need people who are able to flourish in a trusting, cohesive, happy and strong environment that will transcend these qualities to others in a substantially unique way. Doing so can lead to a greater transforming effect on the organization, its customs, processes and productivity.

## BEHAVIOR STYLE & COMMUNICATION

There is a difference between being a boss who knows the business and drives for results and being a leader who motivates the team to get those same results, because the latter does so by inspiring the team to win together. One strategy to achieving this can be found in the way the organization, plans and communicates.

The communication gateway between a leader and their team is the most important door you will ever open as a leader. It is accomplished by carrying out the leadership traits in a manner that invites some level of 360 degree encouragement.

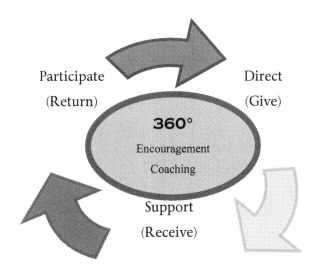

As a leader you have the power to create your own business communications model. Simply put, a business communication model is the design to which you will agree to interact with your team, and vice versa. More than a business coaching model, it is a communications coaching motivator. Designing the method of communication, as the leader allows you and other levels of your business to value the experiences others have and are bringing to the table, all of which will help your business grow and deliver unprecedented results! Serving as one of the spokes in the relationship management cycle, it is holistically intrinsic in nature by giving, receiving and returning valued feedback.

Intrinsic motivation comes from a form of success which helps to make sense of the meaning for life and the lives of others. Quite often a person (leader included) doesn't fully comprehend the value of things, people and places until it's almost been lost. For some strange reason it is easier to see the value of life, leadership and business *after* a few "mistakes" have been made. Nonetheless, personal growth, the taking on of social causes, and making a difference in the world, gives life and business perspective. It puts you in a perspective of being able to categorize value. Congruent with your values as a leader there is also the fulfillment of extrinsic motivations that complete the balance in creating your blueprint for success.

Extrinsic motivations are those having everything to do with personal achievement; awards and recognition. Since you were a tiny tot in grade school you have prided yourself on stars, and stickers, and kudos for the great things you do. There is nothing wrong with working hard and being recognized for it. In those moments of recognition, enjoy it. Don't give excuses as to why you can't, or give energy toward all of the sad experiences you've had to overcome to get there; just smile and enjoy the moment of recognition. Don't be like that woman you compliment about her looks and she responds with phrases like, "this old thing?" or "girl I got this from the dollar store!" Whenever your receive accolades, especially as a leader, there is no better response than, "thank you." Anything more than that devalues yourself and the reward. Devaluing yourself or your accomplishments doesn't add value to your brand as a leader. What it does do, is devalue your power as a leader.

In the world of leadership, discrediting yourself is nothing but a leadership neutralizer; dream killer. A leadership neutralizer is something that happens to prevent a leader's influence negating the leader's efforts. Who would want to follow behind the kind of leader that works hard to then discredit their own worth?

The world around you can shape you for the negative if you let it. To have a sense of self as you go about your business, calls for you to make conscious positive choices, be humble and have tremendous gratitude. Sometimes those choices are really hard, and result in many mistakes. But, no matter what happens you can recover when you change the way you respond; when you allow yourself to be motivated extrinsically. So then, as a leader you must know your value, accept it, and enjoy when it's your time to be celebrated!

Authentic leaders are constantly aware of the importance of staying grounded, even in or after celebration. If anything, celebration is an indicator that you have made progress, but there is still more work to be done. Having a strong personal life makes the difference in staying grounded while succeeding in business. So, there's nothing like receiving a top performer's award at work to then go home and have to vacuum, change diapers, do laundry, clean toilets and cook dinner. It's a great reminder of perspective and staying humbly thankful.

Even so, in addition to family time and personal fun time, another way authentic leaders maintain gratitude and humility is by engaging in physical exercise, spiritual practices and community service (Collins & Porras, 1996). Essentially, you are no good to others if you don't take care of yourself. The equilibrium between the two is what develops certain leadership styles.

## LEADERSHIP STYLES

Are you a transformer? Not the robots of course; the leader. To have a Transformational Leadership style means that you have the ability to inspire followers to trust in your brand enough that it makes them feel like they are a partner in achieving the organizational goals. Do you see others overflowing in your passion for the business in a way that helps the business perform at optimum levels? If so then you are a leader whose style is transformational.

Maybe you're just a super excited individual! There's a place for all of your energy in leadership as well. If that's you, you'd be considered to have a Charismatic Leadership style. A great example of a charismatic leader would be a preacher. Have you ever heard the preacher at church who is delivering a powerful message, but while he or she does so, they are just about screaming from the top of their lungs delivering it? Their enthusiasm gets the crowd going and motivated to support the vision they have painted. The people who attend churches with charismatic leaders, love it, they learn and glean from its energy. While others may feel like it doesn't take all of that to get the message across. So, remember that no matter your leadership style, there are people who need exactly the way you have to offer it.

Another style of leadership is Developmental Leadership. A person who has a development leadership style could very well be enthusiastic like the charismatic preacher in the previous example. However what makes what they do appear different is the methodology behind their presentation. The developmental leader's style tends to be nurturing and growth centric. It is supportive and encouraging toward the followers giving them opportunities to develop and grow. Their style propels others growth by helping them to acquire new skills and see capabilities they maybe have never seen before in their career or business.

Finally there is Transactional leadership. This style of leadership motivates followers by the exchange of rewards for higher performance.

If you noticed, there are various types of leader traits and styles. When creating your blueprint you may want to consider the way you best identify with the traits that best fit and accommodate you, your business, personality, team, and lifestyle. When you find success in what your leadership style is it will attract talented people with whom you can align to the shared goals of the business that together you may create substantial long term results across the various levels of leadership.

## PILLARS OF LEADERSHIP

There are three primary pillars of leadership that give altitude to your effective leadership aptitude. Their development depends upon cumulative wisdom gleaned from your past experiences. The hope here is that you will use these pillars to draw out your blue print and shift your leadership gears to the next level up.

The scientific pillar of leadership focuses on ensuring the planning, labor and technological aspects of your business are led to operate efficiently yet separately from one another. The perspective of this pillar ensures efficient uses of resources are measured, controlled and predictable enough to forecast optimal productivity and resource allocation.

The excellence pillar of leadership focuses on the assurance of quality performance giving confidence to the rest of the organization and its customers and stakeholders. As a catalyst, this pillar of leadership is led to bring out the best in workers by fostering a continuous improvement environment that enhances service level commitments, deepens product development, encourages innovation, is accessible and listens actively to everyone who contributes. Furthermore it engages to discuss and define perspective concerning problem definition and solution to maintain excellence throughout the organization.

The Spiritual pillar of leadership is actually a growing research topic. Researchers are finding that studies show that a direct source of the leader's inner core translates into the business. Have you seen it? Have you ever come across that manager who because they've had a bad day, they make sure everyone else will have a bad day also? Or because of their issues from child from having been mistreated, they mistreat others too? As a leader your inner core, whatever is there, will always shine through everything you do. In other words, your soul will always tell on itself. Thus, there is powerful and implicit, impact of a leader's spirit on decisions affecting their work. The perspective of this pillar supports the leader's pursuit in being comfortable with themselves and conveying these qualities to others through a personal spiritual quest.

## UNDERSTANDING THE FLOW

When you're preparing your blueprint to success you must not exclude the specs of flow; how the pillars of leadership, traits and styles of leadership and so forth all work together. Understanding the flow helps you as the leader to create and employ a blueprint design that permeates growth for you and your business.

The walk of leader can many times feel like a lonely one. People who you thought you could trust find themselves untrustworthy in your book, things that you used to do; like watch television, you don't have time for anymore and so on. In the end, and with great focus, being a leader is rewarding. The object is not to get sidetracked by the distractions, obstacles and roadblocks; which can be people, activities or emotions.

As a leader, when you know your purpose, you'll know other people's, activities and

situational purposes for your life. This will protect
you and keep you from having houseguests all up
in the bedroom; intimate space of your house-
vision; blueprint. The place where they have no
business! In most cases the strongest defense in
protecting your vision is to keep your mouth shut!
When you're excited this can be one of the
hardest things to do! But if you don't, you might as
well plan to leave your front door wide open and
give away every hope you have. In other words,
protect your vision.

Another form of protection is training. Find
out what you don't know about your business.
You can't have just anyone partnering up with you
to build your house. All individuals who will be
partners need to be qualified, certified and
educated in some way in the topics of your field.
It's the only way to preserve your vision and give
it life. Equip yourself. Figure out what you may be
lacking and build on that. Build the skill; build the
business. Be sure to add this to your blueprint
design.

When do you know it's time to take things
to a new level up?

Understanding the flow also involves
knowing when it's time to take your personal and

professional life as a leader to the next level up. You can tell by three things:

... If you feel like your dream is bigger than you. It probably is; which means there is always room to do more; take things to the next level up.

... If when your vision feels stagnant,

... if you've become bored with it all.

If you've experienced or perhaps you are experiencing one or all of these signs now is your time to draw out the blueprint to go to the next level up.

Developing the authentic leader in you will help you to prepare your skills as well as build a solid foundation for your leadership abilities in business.

Think about the basis of your leadership development and style. Then ask yourself these questions:

1. Which people and experiences have had the greatest impact on your life and business?

2. What tools do you use to become self-aware?

3. What does being authentic mean to you?

# INSPECTION

## ...Adding dimension

*I have the courage to manage a successful business.*

# Risk

---

# Chapter 3

Your ascension to success requires an inspection of the tangible and intangible risks in your life.

HOW MUCH RISK IS YOUR DREAM
WORTH TAKING?

All or nothing brings you something; it can either bring you to places of success or places that deflect it. Risk assessment in business starts with evaluating your risk appetite. Measuring your risk appetit determined by how hungry you are for what you're trying to achieve. Then how deeply you believe it can happen and what you're willing to give up for you to obtain it.

## WHAT ARE YOU GIVING UP?

Are you giving up your faith? With God all things are possible! And with prayer and meditation, you will be unstoppable. You can't give up your faith! Anything and everything you can believe God to do, happens with faith and is an essential aspect of blueprint creation.

Are you giving up your positive self Image? Posting irrelevant or inappropriate pictures on social media is a sure fire way to show everyone that you do not value your image over the goals of your business. What you believe about yourself can be very different than what other people believe about you. Which is why it is so important to always present your best foot forward; you won't be able to fake this one. What you feel will show up in everything you do. Furthermore believing the judgments of others can have the same effect; become your setback. Accepting your journey with the ability to move forward is essential to beauty. Positive self image is what you believe about yourself. Before you post that picture of your unmentionables, think about what it says about you, your brand, your business, your purpose. Do you look like a leader? If it is contrary to the positive image your business needs you to uphold, do yourself a favor and take it down.

Are you giving up your confidence? Wearing confidence is sexier than anything you could ever take off. Confidence is more than a look; it's a belief of self. Confidence is believing that you can, be, do, and go wherever your mind thinks it can. Confidence is a sense of security in what you hope to happen. It is always forward looking and self improvement focused. Now, confidence sees you there, but courage-gets you there.

Your level of courage is another risk factor to consider. Without it your business is at tremendous risk! Courage is the gas that moves the car from point A to point B. Courage is essential to the beauty of dream manifestation. Giving up on your confidence will have you lose courage and hope. Your risk appetite must be strong enough to disallow the pierce of discouragement to penetrate the hope your courage needs to keep you moving forward.

Are you giving up hope? Hope is the ambition your courage needs to catapult the how part of you reaching your goals. You need to keep your hope alive, no matter the circumstance, dilemma or situation. Doing so keeps you scalable.

Scalability is the perpetual make over-for every area of your life. When something is scalable it is designed to fit and accommodate various molds. In order to maintain scalability, don't give into the busy schedule of not keeping yourself looking good. Looking good is important and in some cases the reason why I client would be interested in working with you. You do want to get your bills paid, right! Don't believe it can happen? I bet you won't get your hair done by a woman, whose hair looks a hot mess, now will you? Of course you won't, because looks matter! The same applies to the image of your business as well! Are you risking scalability?

As your vision and goals are becoming a reality, you'll need to "scale" how you present yourself as a leader, your products and services to fit into where you're going at every stage of your vision. This includes, restructuring your time, getting a new pair of shoes; after all you are headed for the next level up. It includes your diet; how you fuel your vision; what are you reading, seeing, doing to help take your business to the next level up, and lastly it includes staying active, Surround yourself and your business with people, places, plants and things that make you feel alive. Growth is continual so your makeover needs to be a perpetually evolving experience.

Think about your appetite for risk. Then ask yourself these questions:

1. What are the areas you need to grow in or learn?

2. When a new opportunity presented itself what measurement tool did you use to assess it?

3. When was the last time you believed you could do something you never tried before?

4. What's the worst thing that can happen if you actually go for it?

# INSTALLATION

## ...Strategic Mecca

*I am relentless in my pursuit to manage a successful business.*

# *Elevate*

## Chapter 4

It's a good thing that there isn't a magic cookie cutter approach to leadership. If there were, there would be nothing original. Originality builds success.

The success of your dream is not dependent upon you alone. Instead it is co-dependent to a team; a trusted group of people that will be committed to helping you achieve your dreams. Your dreams can be made or broken based upon the support (or lack thereof) you have around you. So, who's on your team?

## TEAM BUILDING

Maybe you don't have a team. Or perhaps you have no idea what kind of qualities you should be looking for in a team. Beyond titles, your team needs to encompass certain character traits. Your team comprised of a Cheerio sized circle (small group) of people help you to not only awaken the dream within but are purposed to be in your life to help keep your dream alive. Every leader needs these qualities in their space. The careful selection of these individuals who will be closest to the intimacy of your dream, your goal, and your heart preserve the vision and develop your leadership personality qualities. In matters of blueprint preservation, here are some key players (and attributes) that you may want to consider looking for in your "Cheerio" team:

The Visionary.

The visionary is the person who can see your dream in its entirety. It's like God has given them access to what He put inside of you. This person has the insight to see your dream in the present and future tense.

They are a forward thinking individual who recognizes the importance of your dream far beyond the birth of its idea. Find her and keep her close!

The Executor.

The executor is the person who goes above and beyond in support of the actual vision of your dream. She doesn't even charge you for her services, she just feels called to help. This person has vested interest and intellect to research, recommend, and document the strategic steps needed to make your dream come alive. With excitement and poise they ensure and exhaust the potential of every task; making sure it gets done so you can focus on leading.
The Doer.

The doer is the person who does exactly what they are told. She's the woman who is probably a leader in her organization and only makes time to help with what you need. And she will never deviate from the plan.

The Timer.

The timer is the person that helps to keep your progress on track. She's the friend that reminds you of your milestones with the perspective of helping you to remain on task. She's a little pushy, but in a good way because her primary objective is to help you complete your vision/awaken your dream within the timeframe you told her you wanted to do it in. She serves as the sole member of the dream dying prevention team.

The Primer.

The primer is the person who cheers you on. Everything you do she celebrates. She is the gal who knows how to creatively pull out the best in you and for you to lead your team in peace and excitement.

The Challenger

This is the lady who is your logical sounding board through strategic input and prayer. With carefulness and a positive attitude she challenges; gives you something to think about while motivating your change process.

If you're not sure if your team has any of these key players, take a moment to consider your surroundings and ask yourself these questions to help you determine, "who's on your team?"

Each one of these team mates might fit the bill of some of the women you call friends. Keep them close. They are special and important to dream preservation. Do not take their presence lightly; they all have a purpose in your life. You may also find that these players might be different people over the course of your business life. That's ok. It's what they add to your life that you must always focus on valuing. Ultimately their mission is to help get you ready to get out there! And no one will know who you are or what you have unless you get out there!

Based upon the PLANICURE© Coaching program created by the Beauty and Business Training Institute, there is a plan you can follow that alongside these players will help get you started to getting your business out there.

After you've removed your old way of thinking and are looking at the bareness of your business there will be a need to position yourself for the next level. Your preparation to positioning your business to get to the next level includes a cutting! In the sense of an actual manicure, you can't get much done if your nails are too long. You may even be a person with naturally strong nails. However, while your nails may grow strong and quick, they may also grow uneven; they too will need to be cut. Cut back on the things that put you out of a ready position. Whether it is people, money, time, or other resources, cut the excess.

What about how is your business labeled? If you don't make sure that your business, product and services are attractive you won't produce any sales. And if you're not making any money, you will go bankrupt and lose your business and impact your quality of life. One of the most frustrating places to be in is to have loads of ideas and not understand where they belong in the scope of your business. Labeling is about giving your business order, or in some cases re-order. It is about categorizing your products and services so that you can regroup their attractiveness and create synergy throughout your entire brand. This type of cutting includes you reviewing your business look.

While you may have analyzed your business look, you must not neglect the metrics and analytics of your business operations. When you review your business operations effectively what it will bring you to ask yourself, whether or not there is a better way to achieve either the same results or improved results. With technological advances giving way to faster and global access to resources, processes and more, you may need to consider ways to streamline your operations. Consider the HOW piece of what you're doing. Is your overhead costly? Are those costs necessary? Can you get it done quicker somewhere else? Do you need to pull a group together or do you do it yourself? The review of your operations may require you to do less so you can do more, meaning you may have to delegate. Hiring help for an entrepreneur can be challenging. After all this is your business, passion, it is the baby you created, right? While this is all true, in the realms of business success, there is no room for glorified leadership that doesn't direct. Leadership with no followers is just a brisk walk. So don't be afraid to delegate as necessary. You don't have to make this dream come alive, alone.

Moreover, analyzing should reveal the areas of your operations that can save you money, increase your time which can ultimately increase opportunity with a healthy return on investment. If you can't do it yourself, or it doesn't make money, its excess- cut the excess and hire some help!

Just like in a manicure, the cutting isn't meant to hurt you. All you are doing with cutting is eliminating waste! You're getting rid of what's overdue and out of shape by removing the obvious. When you are getting a manicure and they put your hands in warm water for soaking both your skin and nail are being cleaned and lifted. The nail soak provides a deeper level of conditioning to the skin in a way that ensures all callous and dead skin is removed. And if they are not removed they have now been lifted for easy cutting. Your nails can't grow if something dead is blocking the flow. The same applies for your business.

Nurturing and lifting, is about deep cleaning. It's the magnified perspective. It's quite anal to be exact. But what it will reveal is the lift factor. It will show you a few more things that can stand to be cut. So with your glasses and a fine tooth comb zoom in; look closer at your business. What do you see? What does your businesses full potential look like? Do you see ways you can clean and lift your business to the next level? Is it in your look, operational structure, product or service offering, your network, your money, your clientele? Where and what is your lift factor?

For the rest of the PLANICURE© model you can purchase the Coaching program. In the meantime, there is a secret you need to be hip to . . . it is the secret formula to successful entrepreneurship.

## HABITS OF A SUCCESSFUL ENTREPRENEUR

The secret formula to successful entrepreneurship is in the discipline of leadership. Within this discipline, there are ten habits successful entrepreneurs have.

**The ability to recognize the power of vision.** Seeing is believing, no really, it's not simply cliché. Seeing yourself and your business at the end result/goal/status/position, etc . . . gives you ownership and a responsibility to bring that vision to fruition.

**The ability to decide to commit.** Having a sense of urgency and rushing are two different things. While the may be related, their precepts are identifiably separate. A healthy sense of urgency recognizes the need to put your product out as quickly as possible and will typically have spelling errors, misprints, flaws in design feel and reflect poorly upon your image. Sure there are times you might feel like throwing in the towel. But in every step of your journey you must decide not to give up or give in.

**The ability to invest in yourself-TIME & MONEY.** Everything has a price and anything worth having cost something. Count the cost and make whatever investment is required. You and your business are worth it.

**The ability to build relationships.** Building relationships is not exclusively equivalent to building a network. This tip refers to building power relationships. Your power circle needs to have in it a few people that you can lean in on for advice, empowerment and most importantly for that gentle nudge to keep you on your game. Evaluate your current circle and adjust accordingly because the balance of your circle is not just about what you can get out of   LEWIS about what you are putting in to it. Be the one who brings someone else higher while also being the one that can be brought to the next level.

**The ability to stay POSITIVE.** While it would be easy to live in a land where the air always smells like tulips, words taste like gumdrops and everything always goes your way, that's not reality. Reality is, sometimes you have to encourage your own self. There may be times where rejection has blocked your view of seeing alternative possibilities in the face of no. Despite the facts, you've got to find a way to stay positive. Maybe it's just a nap you need, or to pull out your journal and write. Whatever the vice, find a way to refocus and remain positive. You may be your only fan-cheer yourself on.

**The ability to be FLEXIBLE.** What about when it doesn't go your way? Well this happens often. But it doesn't necessarily mean you are doing something wrong. It might even mean the opposite! This is why being flexible is important. Don't let your panties get in a bunch. Take a step back and look at the situation from a different angle. Then re-strategize, consider the timing and try again.

**The ability to be RELENTLESS.** You may have thought you went hard yesterday. Gave it your all, eh? That's great! Today, GO HARDER! Every day you must kick things up to the next level. Drive with consistency. Press your way and always keep moving forward.

**The ability to keep a BALANCE.** You are and will be no good to the world you live in or are striving to attain if you're exhausted. Maintaining your momentum will require long nights and countless hours of hard work. However rejuvenation is equally important to hard work. Somewhere in your schedule, build in a time of rest. It keeps you and the vision fresh and always ready for the next opportunity.

**The ability to be willing to TAKE RISKS.** You won't know how great an idea is until you go for it! Don't let the mind gremlins convince you not to try it out. While every idea may not pan out the way you were hoping for it to, there is always one more idea left in the cookie jar. And when there isn't, bake some more cookies! It's that one idea that you think might be a terrible one that propels you to the next level.

**The ability to be CONFIDENT.** Whether or not you believe in your brand, business, and self shows up in everything you do-or don't do. It will show that you don't believe in the vision you've created for yourself. And if you don't believe, then why should anyone else? You've got to find that faith;

belief that it WILL happen, not might, not maybe, not hopefully, but that it WILL. Being confident is also about knowing your worth. Knowing your worth includes knowing the value of your look, design, delivery and pricing. The right persona will value the significance all of that.

# MOVING IN

## ...maintaining the dream

I will take my life to the Next Level Up!

# *Self*

# *preservation*

## Chapter 5

The cool whip to your leadership ice cream sundae is ideology. A strong core business ideology is comprised of your company's values, purpose, and openness to innovation. It is the re-directive energy that initializes creative potential and it comes from rest.

Your core businesses ideology needs to inspire your strategy, creativity and empowerment for your team and your customers. According to a Harvard Business review, Core ideology is proactive, defining the enduring character of an organization in a way that transcends product, market life cycles, technological breakthroughs, management fads, and individual leaders. Most of all it is the vision that builds the company (Collins, J.C., Porras, J.I., 1996).

The flow of Ideation is uninhibited innovative with ideas through prioritization and segmentation. It is not designed in a silo, but rather leans in on the team or network for feedback. Your ideas will birth some type of product whether it is a tangible item or valued service. As a leader those ideas can't flow until you first adopt the ideology of rest.

## REST IDEOLOGY

Successful people are not spending time worrying about "haters," because they are busy living out their dreams, reaching goals and making money! Their focus is always a level up. Even as others move on and move up, their success makes room for ones that are starting to improve what once was. The reason celebrating others will always work to your favor is because as you help and celebrate others getting to their next level, there is now a gap in what was being done. This means there is an opportunity for someone else to fill the need! There's no time for hating, only time to fill in the gaps. Besides, there is enough market for everyone.

Also if someone is doing what you do or wants to do, so what! Don't pout over it. There is nothing new under the sun so the likely hood of someone doing what you are doing or would like to do is great. However it doesn't mean that now you can't do it. NO WAY! The secret is this; YOU make what you do different. Your authenticity is what makes you relevant. Not better, but relevant. For example, pick your favorite singer, or actress, or comedian. Did they stop singing, acting or telling jokes because someone else was already doing it? NO WAY! They made it their own; they made it original and made themselves relevant. If someone has told you or you have somehow convinced yourself that you can't do something because someone else is already doing it, get rid of that thought! Throw it out the window, in the trash. Whatever you do get it out of your head: look up and level up! Spend some time with yourself and find the ways you can do what you do authentically. Whatever you do authentically will automatically be different. There is enough market for everyone- so go and do what you are purposed to do!

## WHAT HAVE YOU BEEN PURPOSED TO DO?

Understanding your purpose understands what you're good at and connects it the vision; what it looks like when you arrive at and operate in your purpose. Then when you understand your purpose as a leader it will be easier to understand your niche. Understanding your niche is what drives your business plan; eventually catering to your business model. It's all about staying in your lane and if there isn't one, creating one. But first you must find your niche.

Finding your niche can take some time. However, once you've find your niche; it may be time to consider the need for revamping your blueprint to fit accordingly.

It's not easy for a business to transform in revamping efforts. The process involves research and tons of trial and error, especially when a transformation; some might call it rebranding, is tremendous. If you're not careful you can go through various stages of product development or removal and still find no new clientele to provide them to! Even if it takes you forever to find the right niche, look for it relentlessly. Don't stop until you've found it. When you find it, you'll know.

My personal journey to becoming an entrepreneur started in my childhood.

For some reason, it felt like there was never any change around when the ice cream truck came by our house. Either that or the answer was always an emphatic, "No" when I asked. My parents had ice cream at home, but it wasn't like that of the ice cream truck, of course. And at the age of 9 years old I decided, I was tired of being told no; I decided that I was going to buy my own ice cream from the ice cream truck from then on.

Off I went into my sister and I's toy box scouting for toys we didn't play with. I only found the ones she didn't play with. I used all of my toys. When I found a good handful, I put them to the side. Then I went looking in my mother's sewing room for extra fabric. She had given us sewing lessons for a few weeks now so, I convinced myself that I was pretty good at it; or good enough.

After lunch that fine sunny summer afternoon, I went back to my room. With the fabric I had taken from my mother's sewing room; royal blue satin with black flowers on it, I sat on the floor stretching out the fabric in front of me. I sat and pondered on what I could make with it. Mom had only showed me how to make dresses for my dolls, not humans. Then it hit me. I had plenty of fabric enough to make a bikini bathing suit. All the teenagers in my neighborhood wore them so I thought it was a great idea and went right to work.

Using a pair of undergarments from my drawer as a pattern, I ran back to mom's sewing room to get her pinking shears. Back in the room I cut out the design and I sewed together the bathing suit bottom. I didn't wear any bra yet so I didn't have a pattern to use for the top; I just gave it my best effort.

Once finished I headed out the door. With my sister's toys and homemade bikini bathing suit I sat out on the front lawn of our apartment building. I placed everything I had neatly on the ground and yelled out "Yard sale" until some buyers stopped by.

My sister ended up being mad at me once she found out and told my parents I sold the toys she had just gotten for Christmas. I got in big trouble for that. But I made $8.00 dollars that day and learned an invaluable lesson. If you want something in life you have two options: accept the no, or use what you have to get what you want.

That same summer I did a play that I wrote, starred in and directed, putting all my neighborhood friends to work as the production crew. I made another $6.00 that day. Needless to say it was a great summer.

Most of my childhood was great, despite some dark days. But even that turned into something. As a part of my healing from those dark days, I started journaling. Journaling turned into poetry and poetry into writing. Later I went on to become an author. Although I worked a full time job, it was fulfilling to write and help others. I enjoyed helping others so much that I started doing consulting work; event planning, organizational re-alignment projects among other leadership designated assignments including review and reorganization of their operational structure and flow amongst other opportunities both on the consulting scale as well as professionally at work.

Before long I started getting feedback on my books and invites to speak at women's shelters family reunion keynote events church events and other non-profit events. I donated countless hours of pro bono services and gave away lots of books away to various causes.

By this time I had finished a degree and got a promotion at work, in the financial industry. So with a bit more knowledge under my belt, I started doing strategic business consulting for small businesses.

Finally years later, I got tired although I was being referred to quite a few clients. It had become overwhelming; plain and simple it stopped being fun. I wanted a change but didn't know quite how to go after it; especially amidst being a wife and mother traveling extensively on business and so forth. So I took a year off from the business of consulting and sat back in lots of prayer and meditation after which I found myself back in school.

Completing my educational pursuits required many long nights of studying, mentoring at work and in my personal life, sleepless nights, business trips, tears, fears, and feelings of emptiness, executive meetings, presentations to government officials, and the pressure to succeed. Everything was moving so fast; maybe even too fast.

One day I was happy in my job and the next I was dreaming up big businesses and exploring all the ways I could do things differently. I'd go back and forth with that and telling myself those goals were impossible to achieve; the ambitious little girl inside me was long burned out.

Until I finally realized, "what do I have to lose?" So I stopped chasing the dream of

100

someone else's success and made up my own. As years passed, day by day I learned more about myself, how to take care of me and my family and started enjoying life again. I figured out that my success wasn't going to look like I thought or how anyone else thought it should look. And surely I had no idea how to make sense of everything I had been through. There were just too many irons to that fire. So, I narrowed things down and allowed my talents to flow into two categories; Writing (books, songs, plays; anything) and Coaching/Development.

What's my point? My point is that where you are now may not look at all like where you are going. The lesson to be learned just wasn't about getting ice cream from the ice cream truck. God birthed something greater in me; purpose. So, in the meantime and in between time don't relinquish your small beginnings. Be careful not to let the process of arrival no matter how convoluted or small it may seem to look, convince you to quit because it will all make sense when it's supposed to.

## ARE YOU IGNORING THE VOICE INSIDE
## OF YOU?

What could God do in your life if you could just be ok with the package he delivers your destiny in?

If you could have the foresight to see that your success was going to look different than you had planned. Would you still be willing to grow, climb, achieve, conquer and win in season and out?

The capacity to bring the imagination of an idea to life is what distinguishes a leader from others; it's the guts, the gall to get there. Your life and business success are dependent upon your obedience to the call and willingness to create a blueprint for it. It's the very act of yielding to what was put inside of you that catapults you as a leader to soar toward your destined purpose. At all costs, you must obey. Why must you obey? Because your happiness in life contends upon it.

Sure you can get another job, but you won't be happy doing it. Not only does yielding to the obedience of the call allow for the laws of attraction to bring you access to the people, places, and resources you need, it also allows you to serve your audience. Yes, serve; leadership in any capacity is a service to whatever body of people are following your exercise of influence. The extent to which you exhaust your leadership skill is what will separate you from being a basic leader from being an extraordinarily authentic leader.

Up to this point, you may have tried everything you thought you could imagine. Now is your time to . . . try again. Then after that, try again, and after that . . . you guessed it: try again! Keep trying, tweaking refining and, adjusting, until you get on the path to where you're trying to go. You will get there. The combination of having a beautiful business and a beautiful life as a leader is more achievable than you think. Once you get a firm grasp on developing a healthy business mindset, authentic leadership style and openness to innovation and taking care of yourself, you can find yourself in a place of peaceful and excellence; the strive for knowing better and then doing it with excitement!

*"You must maintain the excitement of
reaching your goals. It will be the boost you
need in the face of oncoming obstacles and will
preserve the journey toward making your goal
a reality." ~Yolanda Lewis*

Make your blueprint worth living so
you can take the confidence in your
leadership, life, and business to the next
level up!

# Need a speaker for your next event?

Send booking requests to:
Extreme Overflow Enterprises
P.O. Box 1184 Grayson, GA 30017
Or
by email: info@extreme-overflow-enterprises.com

# BECOME A CERTIFIED LEADERSHIP COACH?

Register for the next
Women's Leadership Coach Certification!

*Style. Essence. Greatness.*

www.beautyandbusinessinstitute.com

# Don't miss these other fascinating titles by:

## YOLANDA LEWIS

## Available for order at:

www.extremeoverflow.com

## IF YOU'D LIKE TO CONNECT
## Join the Conversation!

Facebook: www.facebook.com/TheYolandaLewis
Twitter: @y_lewis
IG: ylewis_eo
Website: www.theyolandalewis.com

# References

McMinn, M. R. (1996). *Psychology, theology, and spirituality in Christian counseling.* Carol Stream, IL: Tyndale House.

George, J.M., Jones, G.R., (2008).*Understanding and Managing Organizational Behavior.* Pearson, Upper Saddle River, NJ

Collins, J.C., Porras, J.I., (1996). *Harvard Business Review Magazine.* Harvard Business School, Boston, MA Retrieved from http://hbr.org/1996/09/building-your-companys-vision/ar/1

Glamour Magazine (June 2014) *Do you have what it takes to start a business?* New York, NY www.glamour.com

Bahadori, M. (2012). The Effect of Emotional Intelligence on Entrepreneurial Behavior: A Case study in a Medical Science University. Asian Journal of Business Management 4(1): 81-85, 2012

Founders Institute (2014). What makes an Entrepreneur? Retrieved November 20, 2014 http://fi.co/dna

Bureau of Labor Statistics, U.S. Department of Labor, Occupational Outlook Handbook, 2014-2015 Edition, Top Executives, Retrieved November 20, 2014 from site: http://www.bls.gov/ooh/management/top-executives.htm

Ehrhardt, M., Brigham, E. (2011). Financial Management Theory and Practice, 13th edition. South-Western Cenage Learning. Mason, OH

Hines, H. G. (1973, December). Cross-cultural differences in two-factor motivation theory. *Journal of Applied Psychology,* 376.

Hofstede, G. (1980). *Culture's consequences: International differences in work-related values*. Beverly Hills, CA: Sage.

Hofstede, G., & Bond, M. (1984, December). Need for the synergy among studies. *Journal of Cross-Cultural Psychology*, 419–420.

HKTDC (2008). Extract from Guide to Doing Business in China. Retrieved on September 13, 2012 from site: http://info.hktdc.com/chinaguide/7-2.htm

Wachowicz, J., Van Horne, J (1996). *Fundamentals of Financial Management, (12th ed.)* Wachowicz's Web World: Web Sites for Discerning Finance Students from site: http://web.utk.edu/~jwachowi/wacho_world.html

Keen, Dan 2011, Valuation of a Small Business . Retrieved on September 7, 2012 from site: http://www.ehow.com/about_7441400_valuation-small-business

Bureau of Labor Statistics, U.S. Department of Labor, *The Economics Daily*, Hires and quits increase in September 2014 on the Internet http://www.bls.gov/opub/ted/2014/ted_20141114.htm

38377803R00066

Made in the USA
Charleston, SC
05 February 2015